W9-DGK-003

Note to Parents and Teachers

The SCIENCE STARTERS series introduces key science vocabulary and concepts to young children while encouraging them to discover and understand the world around them. The series works as a set of graded readers in three levels.

LEVEL 3: READ ALONE
These books can be read alone or as part of guided or group reading. Each book has three sections:

• Information pages that introduce key concepts. Key words appear in bold for easy recognition on pages where the related science concepts are explained.
• A lively story that recalls this vocabulary and encourages children to use these words when they talk and write.
• A quiz asks children to look back and recall what they have read.

CRANES, SCALES, and SEESAWS looks at BALANCING. Below are some answers and activities related to the questions on the information spreads that parents, carers, and teachers can use to discuss and develop further ideas and concepts:

p. 7 *What other animals need to balance well?* Ask children to list animals in groups, e.g. forest animals, mountain animals, minibeasts. Encourage them to watch wildlife: squirrels, cats, and birds all use their tail to help them balance.

p. 9 *What happens if you push a domino over?* When one domino falls over it knocks over the next one, which pushes over the one after that, and so on. Ask children to think of other objects with a narrow base that fall over easily, e.g. bowling pins.

p. 11 *How could you use a lump of clay to make the pencil pot balance better?* If you put a lump of clay into the bottom of a pencil pot, it will balance better.

p. 13 *What do you think happens if you try to tip the straw over?* Because most of the toy's weight is at the bottom, it will not fall over. When you try to tip it, it stands upright again. This is why a bus has its engine low down, to stop it from tipping over.

p. 15 *Why shouldn't you stand up in a small boat?* When you sit down in a boat, all the weight is low down, so the boat is steady. But when you stand up, you move your weight higher up, and it is easy to tip the boat over.

p. 17 *How could you balance three coins against one on a seesaw?* You need to move the three coins even closer to the middle. You could even balance four or five coins against one by moving them closer and closer to the point where the seesaw balances.

p. 22 *What do you think happens when a top stops spinning?* It falls over!

ADVISORY TEAM

Educational Consultant
Andrea Bright—Science Coordinator, Trafalgar Junior School

Literacy Consultant
Jackie Holderness—former Senior Lecturer in Primary Education, Westminster Institute, Oxford Brookes University

Series Consultants
Anne Fussell—Early Years Teacher and University Tutor, Westminster Institute, Oxford Brookes University

David Fussell—C.Chem., FRSC

CONTENTS

Pat wants to become an acrobat,
but can she learn how to balance?

© Aladdin Books Ltd 2008

Designed and produced by
Aladdin Books Ltd

First published in
the United States in 2008 by
Stargazer Books
c/o The Creative Company
123 South Broad Street
P.O. Box 227, Mankato,
Minnesota 56002

Printed in the United States
All rights reserved

Editor: Sally Hewitt
Designer: Jim Pipe
Series Design: Flick, Book
Design & Graphics

Thanks to:
The pupils of Trafalgar
Infants School for appearing as
models in this book.

**Library of Congress
Cataloging-in-Publication Data**

Pipe, Jim, 1966-
    Balancing / by Jim Pipe.
        p. cm. -- (Science starters)
Includes index.
    ISBN 978-1-59604-137-0
(alk. paper)
1. Equilibrium--Juvenile
literature. 2. Equilibrium--
Experiments--Juvenile literature.
I. Title.

QC107.P529 2007
531'.5--dc22

2007009206

Photocredits:
l-left, r-right, b-bottom, t-top,
c-center, m-middle
All photos istockphoto.com
except: Cover tl, 5br, 19t—Jim
Pipe. Cover tr, 22ml—Digital
Vision. 2tl, 6tr, 7tl & mr, 8mr,
9tr, 11tr & tl, 17m, 18b, 21bl,
31tr—Marc Arundale / Select
Pictures. 2bl, 20tr—Comstock.
3, 4t, 8b, 23tl, 31bc—Corbis.
5tl, 12b—Courtesy Scania. 5bl,
7ml—Ingram Publishing. 12tr,
31ml—Courtesy John Deere.
15bl, 26ml—Photodisc. 21mr
—John Foxx. 22b—Courtesy
US Navy. 29tr—Select Pictures.

BALANCING

Cranes, Scales, and Seesaws

by Jim Pipe

Stargazer Books

BALANCE

This man is **balancing** on a surfboard.
Balancing means standing up without falling over.

We can **balance** our bodies. So can animals.

Look at this flamingo. It can sleep while **balancing** on one leg!

Flamingo

We can **balance** an object too.
We can make it more steady.
See how all these objects **balance** well.

Tent
Objects with a wide
base balance well,
like this teepee.

Bus
It is hard for a bus to
tip over because it is
heavy at the bottom.

Long tail
This lizard uses its long
tail to keep its balance.

Crane
A crane uses heavy
weights to balance
it when it is lifting.

WEIGHT

When you try to walk in a very straight line, you use your sense of balance.

If too much of your **weight** moves to one side, you lose your balance and fall down.

Some people can balance on their head or their hands!

In this game, too much weight on one side makes the tower fall over.

This boy is balancing
a book on his head.

This girl is balancing
an apple on
her hand.

This man is
balancing a ball
on his head.

Which of these
do you think is
easiest to balance?
Which is hardest?

A kangaroo uses its tail to
help it balance when it hops.

What other animals need
to balance well? Think of
animals that live in trees
and on mountains.

A WIDE BASE

Try balancing your body. If you stand
on one leg, you soon start to wobble.
It is easier to balance on two feet.

On one leg

On your hands and knees,
you touch the floor in
four places. This **wide base**
makes you very steady.

Things that have a **wide base**
balance well. A pyramid
is a very steady shape.

Pyramid

8

These dominoes are standing on their ends. They have a narrow base.

What happens if you push one over?

A bicycle has two wheels. It has a narrow base. When you get on, it is hard to balance.

A tricycle has three wheels. It has a **wider base**. It is much easier to balance.

Tricycle   **Bicycle**

HEAVY AND LIGHT

Light objects are easy to tip over. It is easy to knock over a house of cards.

Heavy objects need a hard push to tip them over.

Things balance best when they are **heavy** at the bottom. **Heavy** pots stop tall plants from falling over.

Plant pots

Does an object balance better if you make it **heavier**? A bottle half-full of sand is harder to tip over than an empty bottle.

Sand

But when you put a **heavy** lump of clay on top of an empty bottle, it tips over easily.

So you need to add the weight to the bottom of an object to help it balance.

Pencil pot

When you put lots of pencils in a pot, it can tip over.

How could you use a lump of clay to make the pot balance better?

TILTING
AND TIPPING

When something leans over, we say it **tilts**. Sometimes a bus needs to **tilt** a little bit, but it must not fall over.

A bus or truck that is heavy at the bottom balances well.

Passengers must not stand on the top floor of a bus. Why not?

A digger's weight is low down to keep it steady. Its two legs spread the weight wide.

Tilt test

Racing car

Look at this racing car.
It is very close to the ground.

All the car's weight is very low down.
This stops it from **tipping** over easily.

Make a wobbly toy. Ask an adult to cut a table tennis ball in half. Fill one half with clay then stick a straw into the clay. Now stick a paper figure to the straw.

What do you think happens if you try to tip the straw over?

ON THE WATER

A ship needs to be heavy at the bottom to balance well.

If a boat is too heavy on top, wind or **waves** can tip it over.

A buoy is heavy at the bottom to stop it tipping over.

In the past, ships carried heavy rocks so they were heavy at the bottom.

Look at this ship. Can you see the heavy red **keel** that stops the ship from tipping over?

Ship

A lifeboat can stay upright
even in very stormy seas.

Lifeboat

A lifeboat is very heavy at the bottom.
If a big **wave** tips it over,
it spins the right way up again.

A wide boat balances
better in the water than a
narrow canoe. It also helps
if people sit in the middle.

Why shouldn't you stand
up in a small boat?

15

SEESAWS

These children are playing on a **seesaw**. There is one child at each end.

They balance each other, so it is easy to make the **seesaw** go up and down.

What would happen if there were two children at one end and only one at the other end?

The shapes on a hanging mobile balance each other.

Seesaw

This boy has made a **seesaw** using a ruler. With two coins on one end and one coin on the other, the **seesaw** tips over.

1 coin   2 coins

Balancing coins

When the boy moves the two coins nearer the middle of the **seesaw**, it balances!

Everything has a point where it balances. On a **seesaw**, this point is in the middle.

Make your own seesaw using a ruler and coins.

How could you balance three coins against one?

SCALES AND CRANES

A **scale** is like a seesaw. When its two sides weigh the same, the **scale** balances.

When one side is heavier, that side goes down.

Are bigger objects always heavier? Think about a tennis ball and a balloon. Which one weighs more?

Old scales use metal weights to weigh things.

Scale

Cranes pick up heavy loads and lift them into the air. A very heavy load could make a **crane** tip over like a **scale**.

But a **crane** has heavy weights at the opposite end to help it balance.

Lots of other machines need to balance. The big arms on this fairground ride balance each other.

HIGH UP

Acrobats can walk along a tightrope, **high** above the ground.

The heavy pole helps them balance. It adds weight low down. If an acrobat tips over on one side, he lowers the pole on the other side.

When you put out your arms, they help you to balance.

Acrobats on a tightrope

A monkey uses its tail when it climbs. When it tips to one side, the tail moves to the other side to keep its balance.

A parrot on a branch or **high** wire uses its tail to help it balance, too.

A potato is hard to balance on its end.

But if you stick two forks into the potato like this, it will balance!

The forks add weight low down.

21

WHEELS, WINGS, AND ROTORS

When a **wheel** spins, it can help an object balance.
A bicycle is hard to balance when it is not moving.

When the **wheels** are moving, it is much easier to balance.

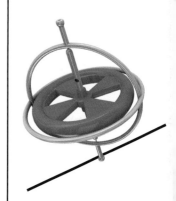

A spinning gyroscope can balance on a thin wire.

When a top spins around and around, it balances on its end.

What do you think happens when it stops spinning?

Flying objects also need to balance. Planes and birds need two **wings**, one on each side.

A helicopter has a big **rotor** to lift it into the air. But the **rotor** also makes a helicopter spin.

A helicopter needs a small **rotor** on its tail to stop it from spinning.

Plane

Helicopter

Rotors

I'M JOINING THE CIRCUS!

Look out for words to do with balancing.

Pat is very excited. She is going to the circus with her friends Paula and Danny.

They walk into the big stripy tent. "Our seats are up there," says Mom.

"Watch out," says Paula.
"These steps are steep."
"Hold onto the rail," says Pat.
"It helps you balance."

Bright lights come on.
Clowns rush into the ring.
One clown is riding a unicycle.

"Wow!" says Danny. "It must be hard to balance on one wheel!"

24

Pat loves the acrobats.
She watches how they
use their arms and
legs to balance.

One acrobat stands on
the end of a seesaw.
His heavy friend jumps
on the other end and makes him fly into the air!

One of the acrobats walks along a tightrope.
He is high up in the air.

Mom is afraid he
will fall.
She can't look!
"Don't worry," says
Dad. "That pole helps
him to keep his
balance."

What a great show!
Later, Pat says, "I want
to join the circus."

The next day, Pat goes to the park. "If I'm going to be an acrobat," she says, "I must learn how to balance."

Danny lends Pat his skateboard. "Take off your bag, first," says Dad.

"That heavy weight on your shoulders will make it hard to balance."

Pat begins to skate. But it isn't easy! She soon starts to wobble. "Help!" she cries.

"Don't keep your feet so close together," shouts Paula.

"Keep your feet apart. It will give you a wide base and help you balance," says Dad.

The next day they take turns riding on Paula's bicycle.

Paula has a ride first. It looks easy. But when Pat gets on, she tips over.

"Try going faster," says Dad. "It's easier to balance when the wheels go around."

"I need more wheels," laughs Pat. "Two small wheels at the back will give my bicycle a wide base. It will be easier to balance."

"Don't worry, you will get better if you practice," says Danny.

The children walk over to the playground.
Pat and the others climb up the big spider's web.

"It's like being an acrobat on a tightrope!" says Paula.

Pat keeps her feet wide apart to help her balance. She hangs on tight with her hands.

They take turns to walk along a narrow beam. They use their arms to help them balance.

Some other children are playing on the carousel. Pat and her friends join in.

"Hang on tight," says Dad.

"It's hard to balance on a carousel when it spins around," says Pat. It makes her dizzy.

Pat has a rest then walks over to the seesaw.

Danny sits on one end. Andy sits on the other end.

"Can I sit behind you?" asks Pat.

"Are you sure?" asks Danny.

"Your weight and Danny's could make me shoot up into the air like that acrobat at the circus!" says Andy.

29

When they get home, Pat sees a squirrel in the yard.

It runs along a wire.
It jumps onto the tree.
Then it hangs upside down to drink from a water bottle.

"Its long tail helps it balance," says Dad.

"It's an acrobat," says Danny.

"It should join the circus with me!" laughs Pat.

WRITE YOUR OWN STORY about things that balance or draw a picture showing something or somebody losing their balance. Look around you and see how things balance. You can make a chart listing them.

Object	Wide base	Weight low down	Like seesaw	Tail
Tent	✓			
Skateboard	✓	✓		
Old Scale			✓	
Bird				✓
Tortoise	✓	✓		

QUIZ

What makes this tower fall over?
Which block is safest to
remove so it will still **balance**?

Answer on page 6

Can you think of two things
that help this digger to **balance**?
Why does it need to be steady?

Answer on page 12

How does a pole help a
tightrope walker **balance**?

Answer on page 20

What helps these objects balance?

Crane

Kangaroo

Pyramid

Buoy

Answers on pages 7, 8, 14, 19

INDEX